ACETYLENE DREAMS

FAR BEYOND

ACETYLENE DREAMS

FAR BEYOND

By

SIMON KING

CONSCIOUS CARE PUBLISHING PTY LTD

ACETYLENE DREAMS
Far Beyond

Copyright © 2018 by Simon King. All rights reserved.

First Published 2018 by: Conscious Care Publishing Pty Ltd
PO Box 776, Rockingham, WA 6968, Australia
www.consciouscarepublishing.com

First Edition printed November 2018.

Notice of Rights
This book is sold subject to the condition that it shall not, by way of trade or otherwise, be lent, resold, hired out, or otherwise circulated without the publisher's prior consent, in any form of binding or cover, other than that in which it is published, and without a similar condition, including this condition being imposed on the subsequent purchaser. All rights reserved by the publisher. No part of this publication may be reproduced, stored in a retrieval system, or transmitted in any form, or by any means, electronic, digital, mechanical, photocopying, scanning, recorded or otherwise, without the prior written permission of the copyright owner. Requests to the copyright owner should be addressed to Permissions Department, Conscious Care Publishing Pty Ltd, PO Box 776, Rockingham, WA 6968, Australia, Phone: (61+) 1300 814 115 or email: admin@consciouscarepublishing.com

Limits of Liability/Disclaimer of Warranty:
While the publisher and author have used their best efforts in preparing this book, they make no representations or warranties with respect to the accuracy or completeness of the contents of this book and specifically disclaim any implied warranties of merchantability or fitness for a particular purpose. No warranty may be created or extended by sales representatives or written sales materials. The advice and strategies contained herein may not be suitable for your situation. You should consult with a professional where appropriate. The intent of the author is only to offer information for a general nature. Neither the publisher nor author shall be liable for any loss of profit or any other commercial damages, including but not limited to special, incidental, consequential, or other damages. The author and the publisher assume no responsibility for your actions.

Where photographic images have been provided by the author and people are depicted, such images are being used for illustrative purposes only. Product names may be trademarks or registered trademarks, and are used for identification and explanation without intent to infringe. Conscious Care Publishing publishes in a variety of print and electronic format and by print-on-demand. Some material included with standard print versions of this book may not be included in e-books or in print-on-demand. If this book refers to media such as a CD or DVD that is not included in the version you purchased, you may download this material at www.conscious-carepublishing.com

National Library of Australia Cataloguing-in-Publication entry:
Author: King, Simon 1950-
On The Edge / by Simon King
ISBN 9780987633750 (Paperback)
Rocky Hudson, Editor.

Printed by Lightning Source
Typeset & cover design by Conscious Care Publishing Pty Ltd

ISBN: 978-0-9876337-5-0

DEDICATION

This book is dedicated to those who dream to be different and who use their imagination to achieve their dreams.

PREFACE

Earth Base Controller to Astronaut: Are you receiving this message? Over.

Astronaut: Loud and clear. Over.

Earth Base Controller: What can you see at present? Over.

Astronaut: I see an alien landscape of endless silence and perpetual daylight, with no darkness – nothing like our planet. An unexplored world of changeless horizons. A place that knows no extremes. Over.

Earth Base Controller: Are you ready and able to return to Earth? Over.

Astronaut: I won't be coming home after all. Tell Mission Control that it's for the best. Astronaut Out.

Earth Base Controller: Your message is unclear. Can you please say again? Over.

Earth Base Controller: Astronaut, please respond? Astronaut?...

**** End of transmission ****

This is a book about mysterious sculptured creatures created from our imagination and religious beliefs, about artificial beings moulded as humanoids to portray our uncanny likeness in the fields of art, fashion, entertainment and leisure endeavours. It is also about ourselves.

It is about how humans choose to become someone else through the temporary guise of masquerade and elaborate costume. It ponders the effects of an incessant barrage of celestial debris from passing comets, transient meteors and other space rocks that collide with our atmosphere, occasionally reaching the planet's surface.

It also suggests taking the time in our busy lives to appreciate a never-ending view on a clear day, and the overwhelming silence of nature – to 'smell the roses', and to dream.

CONTENTS

LIST OF FIGURES	IV
THE WONDER OF ACETYLENE	1
GROTESQUES AND GARGOYLES	4
PERSONA	11
LIGHT AND DARKNESS	17
FASHIONISTA	21
DOLLS	26
THE TALKING DUMMY	32
SOMEONE ELSE	36
THE FOG OF WAR	40
COSMIC MESSENGERS	46
UNIVERSAL STARDUST	54
ON A CLEAR DAY	58
REQUIEM FOR A DREAMER	62
REFERENCES	66
BIBLIOGRAPHY	72

LIST OF FIGURES

Figure 1: The Unknown and Uncertain — 3
Figure 2: Gargoyle in waiting — 4
Figure 3: The Grotesque — 5
Figure 4: Is that a grotesque that I see? — 7
Figure 5: The Winged Creature — 8
Figure 6: Beware the Flying Beast — 9
Figure 7: Gargoyle Awakening — 10
Figure 8: Mask of the Satyr — 12
Figure 9: Beware the Gaze — 13
Figure 10: The Ubiquitous Horse Head — 14
Figure 11: The Unusual — 15
Figure 12: The Cheerful — 15
Figure 13: All in the Family — 16
Figure 14: Always Someone Different — 17
Figure 15: In the Darkness — 19
Figure 16: Hocus Pocus — 20
Figure 17: Faceless Child Mannequin — 22
Figure 18: The Fun of Mannequins — 23
Figure 19: Alive Without Identity — 23
Figure 20: Android or Mannequin? — 24
Figure 21: Are You Being Served? — 25
Figure 22: Am I Mended Yet? — 26

Figure 23: The Doll's Gaze	27
Figure 24: The Vintage Doll	30
Figure 25: The Ventriloquist's Assistant	33
Figure 26: New Age Model	34
Figure 27: Who Am I?	37
Figure 28: Jabberwocks	38
Figure 29: Anonymity and the Mask	39
Figure 30: Someone Else	39
Figure 31: World War I Gas Mask	41
Figure 32: Child at Play	42
Figure 33: A Different Vision	43
Figure 34: Pollution of the Future	44
Figure 35: Reaching Out	44
Figure 36: New Worlds	45
Figure 37: Incoming Meteor	47
Figure 38: Disintegration	48
Figure 39: Fireball Shock	49
Figure 40: Meteorite Impact Crater	50
Figure 41: Meteor Shower	50
Figure 42: Nightfall	53
Figure 43: Stardust Trails	54
Figure 44: The Beginning	56
Figure 45: The End	57
Figure 46: I Can See Forever	58
Figure 47: The Endless View	60
Figure 48: Not Coming Back	61
Figure 49: Tropical Isle at Sea	63
Figure 50: Am I Still Dreaming?	64

Figure 51: Finding Your Way 65
Figure 52: Many Dreams 76

THE WONDER OF ACETYLENE

It's better to burn out than to fade away
It's better to burn out 'cause rust never sleeps[1]

Neil Young and Crazy Horse
My My, Hey Hey and Hey Hey, My My (1978)

The world of personal dreams is an ephemeral state of mind, suspended somewhere between an active imagination and your inherent sense of reality. As a reasonable metaphor, think of acetylene gas and its natural properties.

It is a colourless, highly flammable or explosive gas, with a characteristic faint, sweet, ether-like odour when in its purest form, but a distinctive garlic-like odour (due to impurities) in its industrial form. An enigmatic substance, much like a dream: sweet, imaginative thoughts 'in its purest form', but with the potential to be explosive and malodorous in vivid and harsh reality.

Pure acetylene can be very unstable and highly dangerous to handle (so are some of our dreams). As a gas, it burns readily when mixed with oxygen with an intensely hot and bright flame[2] (3,300°C) and is the third-hottest natural chemical flame[3]. Burn ever so brightly but ever so briefly, and this is reality exposed. If you are going to dream, then make it worthwhile whilst it lasts.

Poet Sara Teasdale may have contemplated such a fatal dilemma in her 1907 poem *The House of Dreams*:

> 'I built a little House of Dreams,
> And fenced it all about,
> But still I heard the Wind of Truth
> That roared without.
>
> I laid a fire of Memories
> And sat before the glow,
> But through the chinks and round the door
> The wind would blow.
>
> I left the House, for all the night
> I heard the Wind of Truth; —
> I followed where it seemed to lead
> Through all my youth.
>
> But when I sought the House of Dreams,
> To creep within and die,
> The Wind of Truth had levelled it,
> And passed it by.[4]

Acetylene dreams can conjure the most splendid thoughts about the unknown or the inconceivable, albeit for a brief, flickering period in our imagination. Such dreams are destined to be fleeting and intense.

'I like the night. Without the night, we'd never see the stars.'[5] This incisive quote from American author Stephenie Meyer speaks of facing the dark in order to experience the wonder of the stars and overcome any apprehension; for dreaming is fostered in darkness.

Darkness has many connotations: from the gloom and blackness of the physical world deprived of light, to a sense of malevolence, of evil, or the foreboding of dread featured in literature and religions. The meaning may be largely subjective to some and not to others.

THE WONDER OF ACETYLENE

Acetylene Dreaming is about understanding the strange and occasionally bizarre elements of life on our planet, and, to an extent, defining such behaviour. It is about appreciating various iconic cultural creations and inventions, from mannequin dummies, dolls and ventriloquial figures, to vintage gas masks and mysterious gargoyles. It is about the transient nature of meteors entering our atmosphere, and their subsequent catastrophic impacts on Earth; the silent, almost continuous rain of foreign bodies and celestial debris.

Figure 1: The Unknown and Uncertain (© Shutterstock)

GROTESQUES AND GARGOYLES

...the gaping, toothed mouth, and the bulging, open eyes, terrible in appearance... The total aspect is grim and repellent... a most horrific image, intended to intimidate the most potent forces of darkness that might beset the building and those who frequented it...[1] – A Grotesque Terror

Ronald Sheridan and Anne Ross,
Grotesques and Gargoyles (1975)

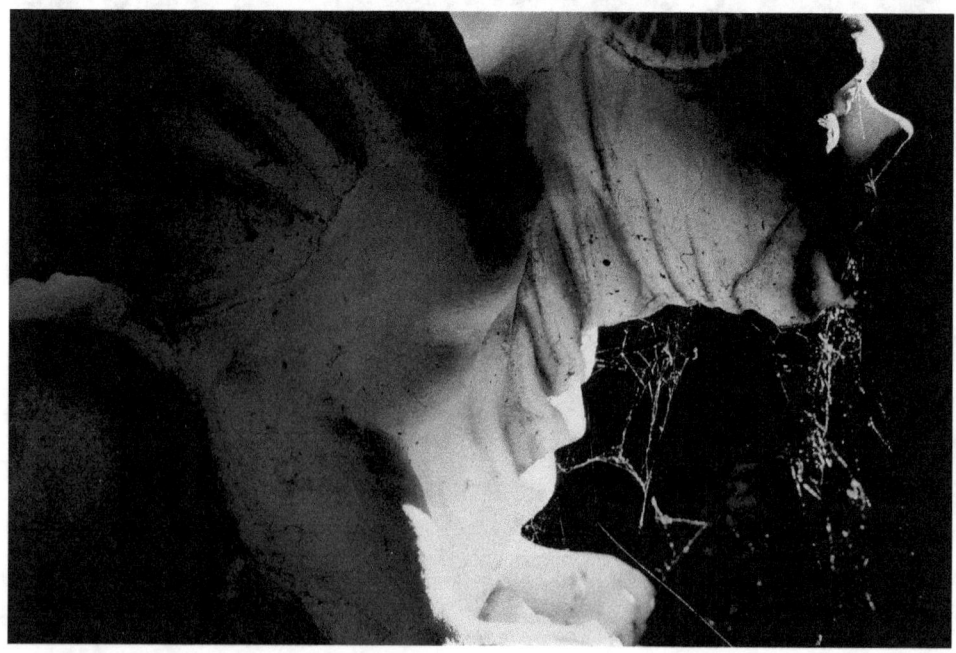

Figure 2: Gargoyle in waiting

GROTESQUES AND GARGOYLES

If this succinct description of an ornamental gargoyle adorning the decorative facade or projected from a prominent buttress of a magnificent towering building seems outlandish, think again. Gargoyles shaped in human form, animal form, or some combination of the two have been a constant presence over many centuries, becoming widespread in the Middle Ages (500 A.D. to 1500 A.D.).

Gargoyles (likely translated as "gullet" or "throat" from the French *gargouille*[2], or "to gargle", as in the gurgling sound of water, from the French *gargariser*[3]) were commonly acknowledged as ancient architectural means to divert rainwater off building roofs in multiple places; they are protruding waterspouts that 'throw water clear of walls' through their open mouths. Thus, these elaborate 'gutters', usually elongated to better direct the water outwards, served a practical purpose: to minimise potential water damage to the structures of the ancient civilisations of Egypt, Etruria, Greece, and Rome.[4]

Figure 3: The Grotesque (© Shutterstock)

However, it is the decorative sculptured 'gargoyle', known as a *grotesque*, that warrants closer scrutiny and probably fascinates us most of all.

Grotesques are not rainwater spouts, nor are they merely ornamental sculptures (*chimeras*). In fact, they are an imaginative, if peculiar, art form conveying a distinctive message, and known in architecture as carved stone figures (or the less common formed terra cotta and metal figures). 'Grotesques are a close, almost identical, cousin of the gargoyle.'[5] The difference is that many grotesques portray an image intended to frighten, intimidate, or threaten the observer.

This could be achieved by combining parts of different animals, or mixing elements of animals and humans, or simply carving some unspecified fantastic species in various postures.

There are several viewpoints on why these imaginary creatures have been created and feature prominently on so many buildings, particularly cathedrals and churches.

In the Medieval era, placement of such visually malevolent sculptures (symbols of sin) on the exterior of places of worship suggested that 'evil' dwelt outside of the church; the building itself offered potential sanctuary to likely parishioners. 'How better to enforce church attendance and docility than by providing a daily reminder of the horrors to come.'[6]

Another viewpoint suggests that placing such bulky stone beasts above any openings into a building (doors, windows, even fireplaces), or high on rooftops, provided a means to frighten away malevolent forces or perceived evil spirits from the premises.[7]

Superstition can be a powerful deterrent, especially when it is assisted by a fearsome and ghastly creature. Grotesques can be sculpted as an embodiment of our nightmares, illustrating many terrifying features of an anatomy best left to our subconscious.

For another perspective, we note that not all gargoyles were terrifying or repulsive. Stone mason carvers and other craftsmen also produced architectural carvings that were designed to amuse or appeal, thereby adding

GROTESQUES AND GARGOYLES

Figure 4: Is that a grotesque that I see? (© depositphotos)

another level of interest to their creations. Gargoyles pulling peculiar faces, exhibiting exaggerated, humorous or mischievous gestures, or just seeming downright odd can also be found on many buildings. A gargoyle's tongue poking out in ridicule clearly sends a specific message to one and all.

For the faint-hearted, however, the following description provides some insight into the macabre of the grotesque:

> '… the ram-horned head. The huge mouth is pulled back and opened, to produce a hideous snarl and reveal the tongue, teeth and fangs… the scowling brow… the pupils of the malevolent… Behind the horns other features appear to indicate a second pair'.[8]

The common elements of many gargoyle creatures include prominent horns, sharp claws, a long spiny tail, and jagged, membranous wings (the wings lend the imaginary creature a touch of realism: aside from its overt

ACETYLENE DREAMS

Figure 5: The Winged Creature

ferocity, it can also fly). These features bring to mind the dragons of medieval lore, or other fantastic and repulsive creatures.

> 'Even after so many years have elapsed, gargoyles carved during the Middle Ages still convey a sense of irrepressible life... gargoyles look ready to use their stone wings to take flight when the shadows darken.'[9]

Now, that certainly would be a disconcerting thought when taking a late night stroll...

So why do many gargoyle sculptures remain fascinating and popular with humankind, despite being created centuries ago? The simple answer may lie in our attraction to the imaginary and the unknown. Grotesques and gargoyles worldwide provide many examples of stone carvings with very few

GROTESQUES AND GARGOYLES

Figure 6: Beware the Flying Beast (© iStock)

design limitations in their extraordinary and bizarre features. Many appear as if they are simply dormant, perhaps awaiting nightfall in order to come to life.

The 21st century short poem *Guardians* by the poet Verana provides some insight into this intriguing subject:

> 'Winged creatures crouching there,
> Longing to glide through the night's air,
> Atop buildings and roofs, we have no proof,
> But some of them seem to move.
>
> They guard by day,

ACETYLENE DREAMS

At night, they play,
Roaming the skies of their home.

While guarding they seem so alone,
The extent of their loneliness is somehow unknown.
They long for acceptance, they long for respect,
So far, not one has gotten it yet.' [10]

Figure 7: Gargoyle Awakening (© Shutterstock)

For such a surrealistic and intimidating art form, gargoyles are rarely found in isolation. 'Rather, they are almost always arranged in rows or clusters; their function accounts for their seemingly gregarious nature.'[11] Perhaps when so many of these characters are relatively grotesque in appearance, it is best to congregate after all.

PERSONA

**Life isn't about how to survive the thunderstorm,
but how to dance in the rain.**
            Adam Randal Young
              Musician and Artist

The ancient Greeks worshipped more than sixty gods and were renowned for conducting popular theatrical festivals to honour their deities. The roll-call of immortals is lengthy: there was *Zeus*, the King of the gods and father of men; *Hades*, the King of the Underworld; *Aeolos*, the god of wind and air; *Poseidon*, the god of the sea, earthquakes and storms; and a plethora of others, such as *Pan*, the god of nature, *Ares*, the god of war, and *Chaos*, who reigned over the empty space between Heaven and Earth.

To properly acknowledge supreme beings, classical Greek theatre relied upon various masks created by artisans and used by actors to symbolically portray the Gods. These masks transformed the actor into an effective representation of the mythical being.

Such was the skill and technique of the ancient manufacturer to produce an intensity of gaze, that the mask seemed alive. The power of the mask to capture the viewer lies in its gaze, and '… not in its ability to conceal or identify an individual persona, as in modern time...'[1]

Figure 8: Mask of the Satyr (© Shutterstock)

The power of the mask to transform the wearer and the grotesque face of the architectural figure to impress the viewer is evident in many other ancient cultures.

However, I am most intrigued by the rather curious modern custom of wearing animal head masks for celebrations or other social occasions. We could look to the gods of ancient Egypt for an indication of where such unusual practices may have originated.

Many gods worshipped in the very earliest periods of Egyptian history were often symbolically assigned an animal's head (thus being depicted as part animal, part human), or were commonly represented as an animal and depicted with its specific abilities.[2]

Figure 9: Beware the Gaze (© Shutterstock)

The head of the lioness, cat, cow, baboon, or jackal, and hybrid variations of other animals provided an ample range of such choices. What was good enough for gods in ancient Egypt is probably worth wearing to a social event in today's society. Such prestigious cult images certainly could not be disparaging, after all.

There is also the arcane element and the anonymity attached to wearing an animal head mask, thus turning oneself into a half-human, half-beast for the occasion. The only difficulty lies in selecting the most appropriate animal mask compatible with your personality and disposition.

This can be a complex decision and highly dependent upon the type of social function, the attendees, and the weather, if outdoors. If attending alone, the choices can be many, without fear of competing with others of similar ilk.

Figure 10: The Ubiquitous Horse Head (© Shutterstock)

However, if one chooses to wear an extraordinary or bizarre animal head in order to be noticed in a crowd, it is probably wise to base the decision on a specific creature, such as an exotic dog or perhaps a cute owl.

Figure 11: The Unusual

Figure 12: The Cheerful (© Shutterstock)

ACETYLENE DREAMS

If all else fails, join the crowd.

Figure 13: All in the Family (© depositphotos)

The compulsion to wear an animal head mask to social functions can be due to many reasons: the desire to channel a mythical presence, or to generate a sense of mystery to other guests, the personal thrill of remaining anonymous, or perhaps simply adding irreverence to the festivities through ridiculous camouflage. The art lies in selecting the right mask for you.

LIGHT AND DARKNESS

Marching to the beat of a different drummer.[1]
Henry David Thoreau
Walden (1854)

Figure 14: Always Someone Different (© Shutterstock)

ACETYLENE DREAMS

Every so often someone may come into your life who looks at the world with a totally different perspective; a person who appears to think and act like no-one else. All of us have an inherent degree of motivation to be different, but in a select few, this drive can be significant. As Zimbabwean philosopher and author Matshona Dhliwayo so eloquently states, 'Diamonds do not need anyone's permission to shine.'

Clowns can exhibit remarkable qualities that allow them to shine in their performances, entertaining and delighting audiences. Of course, there are many types of clowns in the world. Character clowns adopt the guise of the eccentric for optimum effect, appearing in circuses, rodeos, stage shows, or at parties and other social functions. As a subtle variation on these comic characters, there are particular clowns who appear downright scary to some adults and to impressionable young children.

There are many reasons why clowns in exaggerated, creepy make-up and costume terrify some of us. To shed some light on this perceived 'clown fear', we could consider two aspects: the clown's physical appearance, and their attitude or character.

Eye-catching, brightly coloured and elaborate costumes are common for clowns and draw attention to their performance. The more extreme the apparel (garish colours, oversize pants and shoes, peculiar clowning props), the more recognisable the clown becomes to children.[2]

Complementing the outlandish outfits with harsh make-up, a vividly multi-coloured wig, and distorted facial features such as protruding teeth, enlarged mouth and glaring eyes, in turn produces quite a potent image.[3]

Circus clowns are renowned for comedic violence ('slapstick'), clumsy acrobatics and other buffoonery that includes falling, tumbling, tripping, and many other entertaining antics. This association of 'comic relief violence' with a distinctively scary appearance could certainly conjure thoughts about the darker side of clowning in some of us.

LIGHT AND DARKNESS

Figure 15: In the Darkness (© Shutterstock)

However, this is not applicable to the vast majority of the world's professional clowns, who provide endless merriment with their joyous routines and comical stunts, amusing and entertaining the viewers without intimidating them. After all, plenty of laughter is still the best medicine for people. As the famous American Shrine Circus tramp clown Al Ross said in his last interview, 'Anyone who can make people laugh has the greatest gift God can give a man.'

Magicians are another group of extraordinarily talented entertainers who rely upon their meticulous artistic skills to conjure magic. In bygone times, sorcerers evoked the dark forces of the mystical or supernatural and employed the special effects of alchemy to produce their 'magical powers'.

Whatever the era or the enchanter involved, people have usually been susceptible to the belief that something spectacular might occur if conjured by a magician, sorcerer or spell-caster. A special person who claims to mysteriously control the forces of nature by use of magical powers will always get your attention.

To elicit such phenomenal results may require the skilful application of certain ancient ritualistic arts. For those with good intentions, white or 'natural' magic is considered to traditionally provide positive results, such as personal well-being, better health and fortune. The dark or 'black' magic is the other side of the same coin, seeking malicious or harmful outcomes, or the bestowing of malevolent powers.

Figure 16: Hocus Pocus (© depositphotos)

Magic is often difficult to explain in terms of actual causes and effects, but does rely considerably upon personal belief and faith in such practices.

> 'Magic exists. Who can doubt it, when there are rainbows and wildflowers, the music of the wind and the silence of the stars? Anyone who has loved has been touched by magic…'[4]
> **American author Nora Roberts,** *Charmed (1992).*

FASHIONISTA

You know, a carving, especially if it's polychrome, is not meant to move. These faces, these half-bodies, when you animate them, they're more live than the living. They can be dangerous for those who don't really understand them. With contained energy, no one can predict what will happen when it's released.

Jacques Yonnet
Rue des Maléfices (1954)

The store dummy, the display mannequin, and the articulated model are all objects serving the same purpose. They are artificial, inanimate creations we use to represent the human form or copy the human figure.

For most, this purpose is to realistically display designer garments, headwear, hair styles, eyewear and everything in-between. Mannequins provide the potential purchaser with the opportunity to view fashion as if worn by an actual person. There are also several scientific uses in studying the behaviour of the human body under various conditions.

The first 'fashion models' were dolls that simulated ideal body shapes and thus portrayed the fashionable standards of the time in the best way (most notably, from the eighteenth century onwards). Dolls provided all the realistic attributes and fine detail essential to model garments.[1]

Before the introduction of 'living' models in the mid-1800s, we had expressionless, functional mannequins; 'the earliest models were generic, charac-

ACETYLENE DREAMS

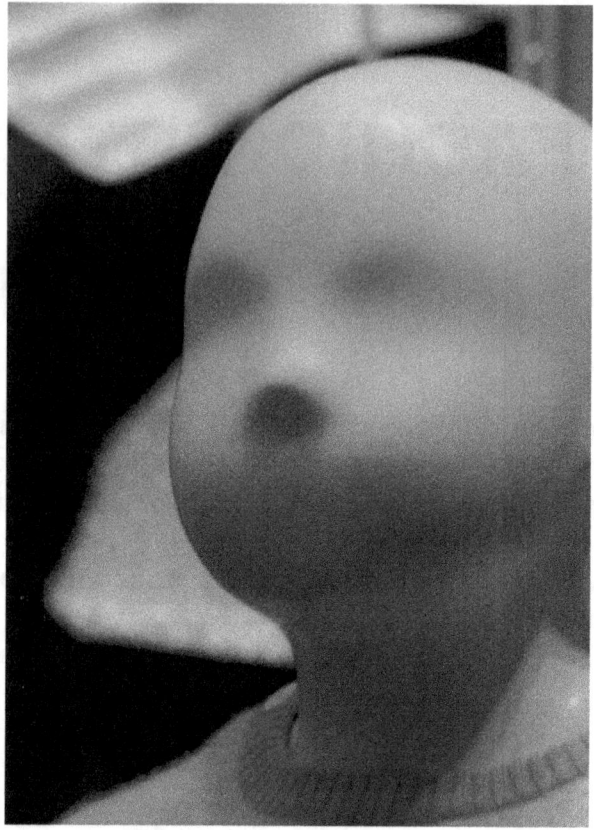

Figure 17: Faceless Child Mannequin (Image credit: Kevin Bilyk)

terless and object-like...'[2]. There were tailors' dummies, life-sized wooden dolls used by artists, and anatomical models for teaching medicine. These representations of the human figure were prepared in various media and did not always achieve realistic features; sometimes they formed only a partial human body, such as a headless trunk or a dismembered torso.[3]

The advent of articulated mannequins with realistic heads, hands and feet, as well as the introduction of diverse and artistic facial expressions, are modern developments that reflect the evolution of technology.

Plastics and the more expensive and realistic fibreglass have considerably expanded the choice of designs. It is now possible to apply fibreglass skin resembling human skin on realistic human faces, or shiny metallic coatings on plastic mannequins. Cool has arrived in the world of mannequins.

FASHIONISTA

Figure 18: The Fun of Mannequins (© Shutterstock)

However, some have still remained dehumanised by face coverings, or headless, or appear '… like cloth dolls or androids on a production line'[4] – they are alive but without personality or identity.

Figure 19: Alive Without Identity (© depositphotos)

ACETYLENE DREAMS

As mannequin technology approaches the realism of humanoid robots or androids, in the foreseeable future it may become increasingly difficult to distinguish them from their advanced robotic counterparts.

It is probably predictable that these inanimate cultural mannequins will eventually become interactive design forms readily capable of illustrating the value of the garments they wear.

Figure 20: Android or Mannequin? (© iStock)

It may also be possible that they could change their own garments to suit each customer, and, might I suggest, even open the door for the customer.

FASHIONISTA

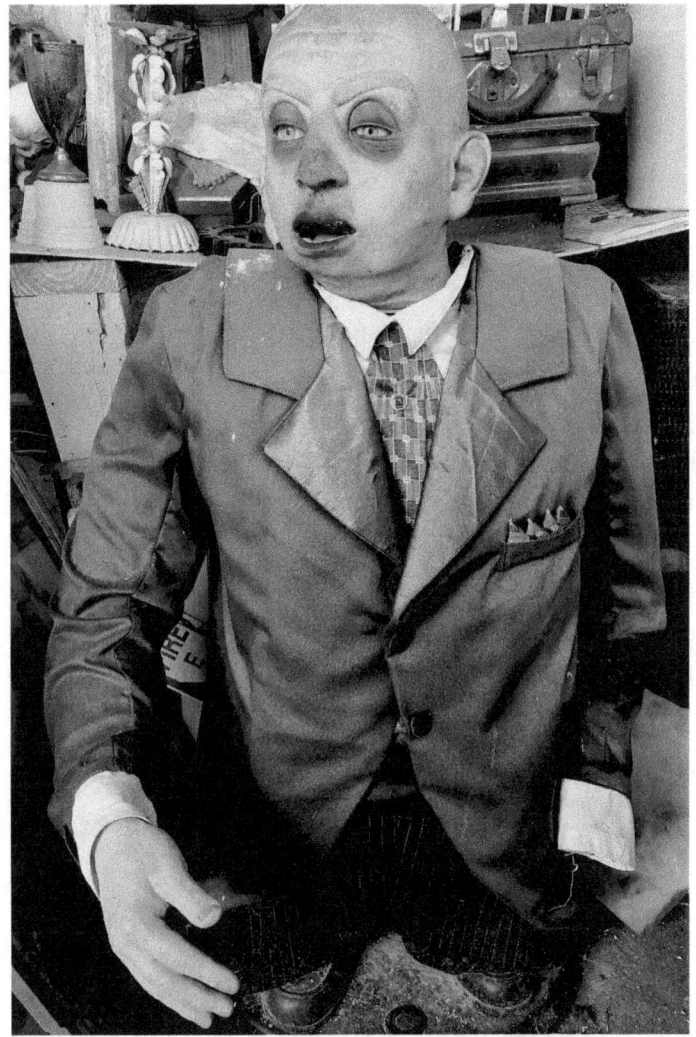

Figure 21: Are You Being Served? (© Shutterstock)

DOLLS

I'm a little doll who was dropped and broken
Falling off my mommy's knee
I'm a little doll who has just been mended
Now won't you tell me please.

Are my ears on straight, is my nose in place
Have I got a cute expression on my face?
Are my blue eyes bright, do I look all right?
To be taken home Christmas Day?...[1]

Melville A. Leven
Are My Ears On Straight? (1953)

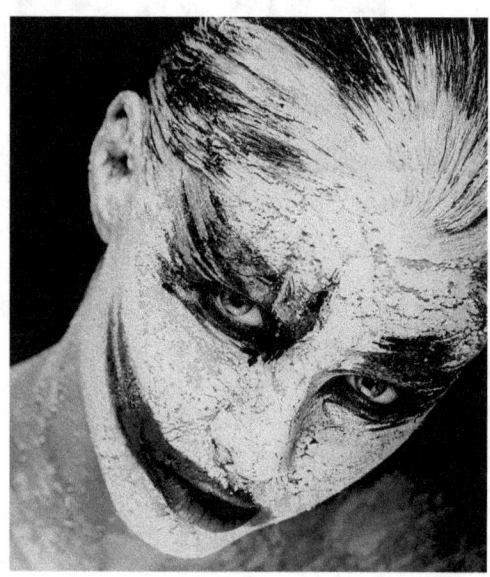

Figure 22: Am I Mended Yet? (© Shutterstock)

DOLLS

Everyone knows what constitutes a doll. The word is thought to have originated from ancient Greek, with meanings such as idol, image, or form; puppet comes from the Latin *pupa*, for puppet and little girl.[2] There are many connotations as well, such as use as a plaything by little girls, for educational means, as spiritual or ritualistic effigies, or for decorative collection, display or entertainment purposes.

Across many cultures and eras, the doll possesses one common feature; a solitary characteristic that separates each doll. To the many children who love such toys, each doll embodies life itself. To the adults who own such art objects, each doll is 'as good as alive'. To those who cast spells and indulge in ritualistic magic, the doll as an effigy is a living spirit.

'The doll is inanimate, lifeless, non-living, dead, yet by way of modernity's own animistic impulse (every natural thing in the universe possesses a spirit or soul apart from a material existence), it also comes to life, is brought to life and possesses the desire for life.'[3]

For most young children who were raised with a doll, the gaze of their

Figure 23: The Doll's Gaze (© iStock)

doll's staring glass eyes cements the relationship. The eyes follow your every movement, sometimes even appearing to glare at you.

For an inanimate object that cannot see or hear and rarely speaks more than a few recorded words, dolls appear to hold quite an important role in a child's life. The following extracts from the extensive poem *Betsy Bouncy Doll* by Canadian author and poet A.K. Ashic (2015) provide a sensible perspective of such dolls:

> 'Little Molly Minden begged her mother, please …
> Could I have a Betsy bouncy doll for Christmas?
> I've been good all year, you see,
> And I really want one, everybody does,
> And if I don't get one, I think I'm going to bust …

> We'll see, we'll see, her mother cried
> Don't bug me about it now
> I'm far too busy to think of toys
> I've other things to do…
> Write it down, make a list
> And later I will look at it for you …

> … Panic started to set in as she went from store to store
> Every one of them was sold out, not one Betsy bouncy doll about
> Oh, the tears that would flow when her daughter started crying
> Christmas would be ruined and not from lack of trying …

> … Well, I guess that's that, there's no point in crying,
> They're all gone, so what's the point in trying?
> And as she got up to leave her heart began to race
> Who could have guessed it would be sitting in that place
> It was a Betsy bouncy doll sitting on the shelf …

> … What joy she felt, what happiness,
> Christmas would be saved and the road to bliss now paved
> Until a hand came down upon hers and ended quickly her dream
> It turned out someone else's mom, thought the exact same thing

> … A fight broke out and Betsy bouncy fell to the floor

Another woman screamed out loud
"There's more of them in aisle four!"
It was a mad frenzy as the ladies fought and yelled
That is until the manager showed up and stopped the brawling bunch
Which was a good thing as Molly's mother was about to take a punch

… Calm down, there's no need to fight
I will make this right
And when it was over, Molly's mother knew she'd won
A smile of satisfaction on her face, she beamed from ear to ear
Christmas would be great this year …

…Then one week after Christmas, the madness long forgot,
She found Betsy bouncy doll lying in the same spot
It seemed that Molly had forgot she'd wanted her so bad
It seems that Molly didn't know the trouble her mother had
How could she have known the folly created by this one small dolly?

Next year, Molly's mother thought, I wouldn't mess about
And if someone tries to fight with me, I'll just knock them out.'[4]

However, for some among us, there can be quite an inexplicable apprehension about certain dolls of near human-like appearance, particularly if congregated on display as antiques in a toy museum. They may be lifeless, but surprisingly, it is those very features – glazed eyes, stern or curious expressions, polished or waxed faces with an aura of remoteness from reality – that most pervade our senses.

If the vintage dolls are awaiting complete restoration, the chipped paint, the hairline facial cracks, a lack of hair, or a defective eye all contribute to this sense of the unnatural. Such dolls may not be outright frightening to most of us, but they can be creepy and unnerving.

Of all the early vintage dolls most popular in the 19th century, considerable workmanship was involved in making dolls with solid wax heads

ACETYLENE DREAMS

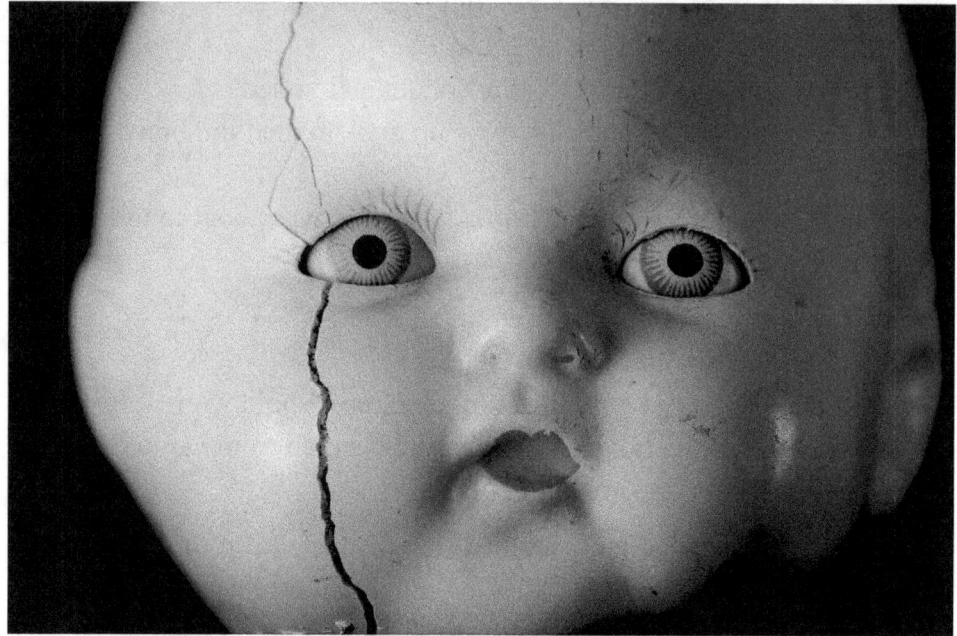

Figure 24: The Vintage Doll (© Shutterstock)

modelled by hand (and subsequently industrially poured), and later, dolls formed of wax over a composition, wood or metal. Usually the head was the only part made of wax, and the bodies of cloth. The most commonly available 'waxed' dolls had a head formed of wax over papier-mâché on a straw-filled cloth body.[5]

Wax presented a quasi-realistic finish for the doll's face, and only enhanced the typical 'smiling-faced dolly'. However, in some cases, their sleeping glass eyes or unique painted facial features would result in a totally different appearance.

Glass pupil-less or all-pupil black eyes could give the rather bizarre effect of an ominous glare, whilst any hairline cracks in the head's wax contributed to the image of oddity. Some dolls also had sawdust-filled cloth bodies, which if inadvertently damaged could release the sawdust, much to a child's dismay.

The poem *My Little Doll* by English professor, historian and novelist Charles Kingsley was originally published in 1863. The following extracts from this poignant fairytale verse succinctly outline a doll's emotional appeal, regardless of its appearance.

> 'I once had a sweet little doll, dears,
> The prettiest doll in the world; ...
> ... But I lost my poor little doll, dears,
> As I played in the heath one day; ...
>
> ... But I found my poor little doll, dears,
> As I played in the heath one day:
> Folks say she is terribly changed, dears,
> For her paint is all washed away,
> And her arm trodden off by the cows, dears,
> And her hair not the least bit curled:
> Yet for old sakes' sake she is still, dears,
> The prettiest doll in the world.'[6]

By the end of the 19th century, a complacency that highly popular unglazed china dolls '... began to look very much alike, no matter the maker' persisted in the doll industry. Hence the manufacture of a new type of doll in the early 20th century '... intended to be as true to life as possible'. The character dolls '... had rolls of fat, dimples, uneven features, and the sulky or even unhappy expressions of real babies'.[7]

In some respects, this may have been the beginning of the *mischievous* look for dolls – grinning, cheeky, unhappy, or almost surly. When coupled with those incisive glass eyes, perhaps they looked a little too realistic after all.

THE TALKING DUMMY

> Jonathan West, ventriloquist, a master of voice manipulation ... with a talent for putting words into other peoples' mouths. In this case, the other person is a dummy, aptly named Caesar, a small splinter with large ideas, a wooden tyrant with a mind and a voice of his own ...[1]
>
> **Caesar and Me**
> *The Twilight Zone (1964)*

The ventriloquist's 'assistant' is an elaborately crafted puppet known as a *ventriloquial figure* or *dummy*, and comes in many shapes and sizes. Although these artificial beings may vary in height from a mere 30 centimetres to that of an adult person, the dummy is conventionally around one metre in size, in order to be seated comfortably on the ventriloquist's knee or in their lap. Early versions were traditionally crafted by skilled artisans in lightweight wood or papier-mâché, although in the modern era a diverse range of new age materials are used.

These puppets are called dummies because they cannot speak on their own (hopefully). However, the dummy's duty is to entertain an audience by 'coming to life' through its handler, as if it were a living entity. There have been many highly successful versions of such dummies in the world of entertainment, with a diverse range of facial and head movements simulating human expressions and mannerisms.

THE TALKING DUMMY

Figure 25: The Ventriloquist's Assistant (© Shutterstock)

Perhaps most intriguing about these characters is their uncanny ability to come to life through artful ventriloquism, so an audience cannot tell the difference between its human handler and the dummy. A dummy can also project a variety of personalities by intricate use of its facial features and subtle head movements. The result is a ventriloquist's assistant able to assume various poses and many attitudes.[2]

The ultimate dilemma about such dummies, as pursued in various works of literature and in films, is whether they can actually talk without the ventriloquist in control. Absurd and fantastic as it sounds, many science fiction and horror programs have proposed just such a fanciful idea, the story line ultimately leading to the untimely demise of the ventriloquist.

The art of successful ventriloquism is to present to the audience an illusion of reality, a temporary deception that the dummy actually speaks and interacts just like another person. Given that the physical appearance of such

Figure 26: New Age Model (© iStock)

artificial dummies in earlier days was sometimes mechanical and even disjointed in body movements, it would be difficult to entertain such a belief.

However, what if the 21st century ventriloquist's assistant appeared almost human, no longer simply a dummy, but a robotic being with artificial intelligence? Would the illusion that it only speaks in front of an audience persist?

A fitting response to such a question may be the following line, uttered by the disgruntled ventriloquist in *The Dummy*, a 1962 episode of the American horror/science fiction television series *The Twilight Zone*: 'Sweet dreams, Willie [the Dummy]. Your next booking is in a fireplace.'[3]

The ventriloquist and the theatrical dummy are inextricably linked by their act in order to thoroughly convince an audience that the dummy may actually be alive. This bond of familiarity is so close that, at times, it almost

THE TALKING DUMMY

seems that the dummy is an extension of the ventriloquist – much like his shadow:

'I have a little shadow that goes in and out with me,
And what can be the use of him is more than I can see.
He is very, very like me from the heels up to the head
And I see him jump before me, when I jump into my bed.

The funniest thing about him is the way he likes to grow –
Not at all like proper children, which is always very slow;
For he sometimes shoots up taller like an india-rubber ball,
And he sometimes gets so little that there's none of him at all.

He hasn't got a notion of how children should play,
And can only make a fool of me in every sort of way.
He stays so close beside me, he's a coward you can see;
I'd think shame to stick to nursie [nanny] as that shadow sticks to me!

One morning, very early, before the sun was up,
I rose and found the shining dew on every buttercup [flower];
But my lazy little shadow, like an arrant [utter] sleepy-head,
Had stayed at home behind me and was fast asleep in bed.'[4]

These eloquent verses by famous Scottish poet, novelist and travel writer Robert Louis Balfour Stevenson are from his 1885 poem, *My Shadow*.

'Ventriloquism is the technique of making others think that your voice comes from somewhere other than you'[5] – an effective *illusion of the senses*. In the theatrical world of live on-stage performances, the role of the 'talking dummy' is to entertain, usually at the expense of the ventriloquist.

The dummy often plays the role of the clever, cheeky and recalcitrant offsider, intent on creating humorous commentary and assorted mayhem:

'My father's name is Ferdinand;
My mother's name is Liza.
So naturally when I was born
They called me Fertilizer.'[6]

SOMEONE ELSE

A mask is what we wear to hide from ourselves.

Khang Kijarro Nguyen
(2016)

It is quite possible to become someone else or something extraordinary for a brief interlude in one's life, by assuming the right physical disguise to effectively conceal true identity. One of the simplest means to transform oneself is to wear an elaborate decorative mask. This type of facial covering has been used over centuries in celebratory festivals and carnivals, religious rituals and theatrical entertainment to camouflage the real person within, whilst enshrouding them in a distinctive aura.

The celebratory mask veils a person, endowing them with a 'false face' as a temporary subterfuge from reality. It provides a rare opportunity for someone to become another, without fear of repercussions or personal embarrassment.

Most importantly for the wearer, the decorative mask permits the inner self to embrace an entirely new character without any inhibitions or doubts. This is confirmed by the numerous and varied etymological derivatives of

Figure 27: Who Am I? (© Shutterstock)

the word 'mask' across many cultures and mythologies.

The common feature shared by these definitions is the element of disguise or transformation of the wearer: *masca* from Medieval Latin for 'mask', 'spectre', or 'nightmare', *más que la cara* from Spanish for 'added face', and *masque* from 14th-17th century French for 'covering to hide or guard the face'.[1] There are also other derivatives suggesting mockery and ridicule applicable to the wearing of the mask.

ACETYLENE DREAMS

Figure 28: Jabberwocks

'... Beware the Jabberwock, my son!
The jaws that bite, the claws that catch!
Beware the Jubjub bird, and shun
 The frumious Bandersnatch!...'[2]
                    Lewis Carroll, *Jabberwocky (1871)*

For the more gregarious, enjoying the moment in a group of mask-wearing devotees would appear the ideal solution for almost assured anonymity.

Figure 29: Anonymity and the Mask (© Shutterstock)

With so many masks available in the world, it could be quite difficult to select our personal preference. More importantly, it may even become harder to actually be 'the person in the mask'.

Figure 30: Someone Else (© iStock)

THE FOG OF WAR

> **Gas! GAS! Quick, boys! – An ecstasy of fumbling,**
> **Fitting the clumsy helmets just in time;**
> **But someone was still yelling out and stumbling,**
> **And flound'ring like a man in fire or lime…**
> **Dim, through the misty panes and thick green light**
> **As under a green sea, I saw him drowning …**[1]
>
> **Wilfred Owen**
Dulce et Decorum Est (1920)

It may seem ironic that the vintage respirators known as 'gas masks', initially developed and used during World War I, remain popular symbols in today's culture.

These innovative tools were designed by necessity, to protect soldiers on the ground waging war in Europe from 1915 (when toxic gases were first used on the battlefield) until 1918. The world had never experienced such lethal fog, intentionally released in warfare to deadly effect.

> '… And when the burning moment breaks,
> And all things else are out of mind,
> And only joy at battle takes
> Him by the throat, makes him blind, …
> … The thundering line of battle stands,
> And in the air Death moans and sings;
> But Day shall clasp him with strong hands,

And Night shall fold him in soft wings.'[2]

Julian Grenfell,
Into Battle (April 1915)

Such protective devices were not restricted to soldiers, with animals operating on the front lines of the battlefield (dogs, donkeys, and horses) provided with suitably modified gas masks.

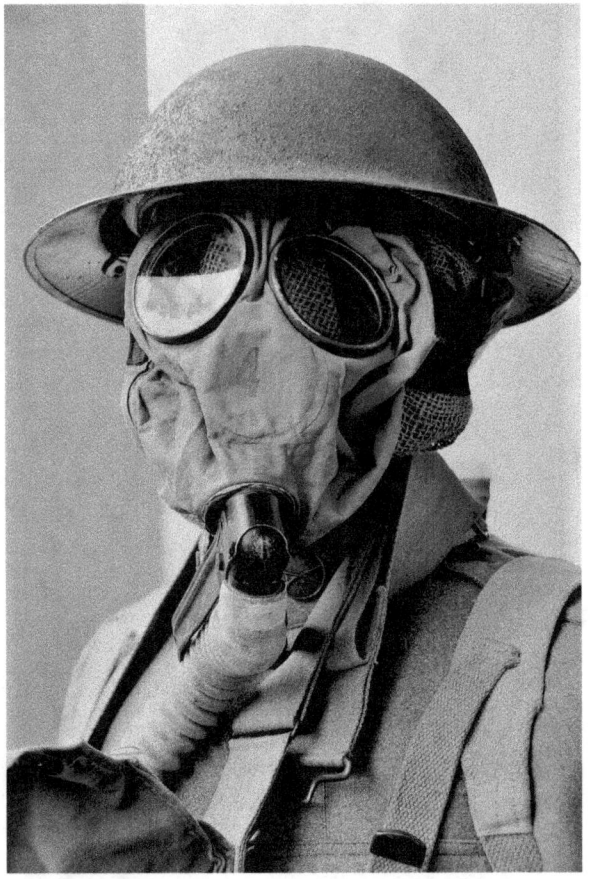

Figure 31: World War I Gas Mask (© Shutterstock)

By the start of World War II, civilians were also encouraged to wear respirators, although there were far simpler versions for the children: 'the type dubbed the 'Mickey Mouse' by virtue of the separate 'google eyes' and snout-like filter casing'[3] was provided to youngsters due to the popularity

ACETYLENE DREAMS

of the cartoon mouse at the time. It was designed to fit children between 18 months and four years of age, the intention being to provide a sense of enjoyment in wearing the mask.[4]

For older children, modified gas masks seemed more appropriate.

Figure 32: Child at Play (© depositphotos)

Gas masks produced to protect the wearers from poisonous gases by purifying the air they breathe have many other interesting aspects to consider. This mask isolates the wearer from the outside atmosphere; when worn, it effectively cuts off most of their senses from the external world, whilst providing a completely different vision of the surroundings.

THE FOG OF WAR

Figure 33: A Different Vision (© Shutterstock)

In the world of artistic creativity, such a mask may represent a symbol of personal entrapment and isolation from one's exterior world outside of the device. It is inextricably linked to environmental pollution and the potential dangers to our eco-system.

As a direct consequence, the gas mask has conceivably come to be recognised as a powerful warning symbol not only of war and world pollution, but of all the other potentially dangerous situations that may arise from them.

ACETYLENE DREAMS

Figure 34: Pollution of the Future (© Shutterstock)

Metropolitan street art and art galleries allow us to distinguish the gas mask as the perfect expression of the perpetual war against environmental pollution, and as a most suitable form of individual protest.

Figure 35: Reaching Out (© Shutterstock)

For others, the gas mask does not always have to represent the sombre or prophetic symbol of danger; it may just be another way to see things differently – perhaps a futuristic symbol of space travel to the unknown environments of new worlds.

> 'We live on a placid island of ignorance in the midst of black seas of infinity, and it was not meant that we should voyage far.'[5]
> **H.P.Lovecraft**
> *(1928)*

Figure 36: New Worlds (© Shutterstock)

COSMIC MESSENGERS

> I saw a star slide down the sky,
> Blinding the north as it went by,
> Too burning and too quick to hold
> Too lovely to be bought or sold,
> Good only to make wishes on
> And then forever to be gone.[1]
>
> Sara Teasdale
> *The Falling Star (1929)*

Suddenly, on a still, moonless, pitch-dark evening, an extremely bright, incandescent glow appears high in sky, above the clouds. The fireball is descending rapidly. It has a long accompanying streak of light, much like an extensive vapour trail, and soon thereafter a thunderous sonic boom follows as the mysterious flying object plummets towards the ground.

Is this strange, alien, fiery body a prophetic messenger despatched by the celestial gods? Could it simply be minute particles of cosmic dust, or large fragments of rock and metallic debris from outer space, vaporising in the upper atmosphere?

In far distant times, such sightings of "shooting stars" might have been considered mythical omens arising from atmospheric phenomena rather than specific interstellar events. But over time, ancient civilisations came to recognise that these meteors were of extra-terrestrial origin by being later recovered on the ground as meteorites.[2]

COSMIC MESSENGERS

Figure 37: Incoming Meteor (© Shutterstock)

'Meteors and comets were seen as heavenly messengers, interpreted variously as the harbingers of death or birth, victory or defeat, famine and drought, or an abundant harvest.'[3] Is it any wonder, given the spectacular skyworks of exploding fireballs, the accompanying thunderous roars, and the daunting blaze of intense light?

In its simplest terms, a meteor is cosmic debris comprising small rocky or metallic bodies (*meteoroids*) or finer dust particles (*micrometeoroids*) from outside of the Earth's atmosphere; it gets incinerated upon entry to this zone. A meteor (or shooting star) is the streak of light produced by a meteoroid as its heats to incandescence due to friction with our atmosphere atoms[4]; the term includes the glowing object itself, and the trail of glowing particles left in its wake.

Meteorites are meteoroids that have survived this passage through the atmosphere intact and reach the Earth's surface.

Just to add an extra dimension, meteors may also be associated with comets passing through the solar system or asteroids and planetoids of sub-planetary mass.

Comets are celestial bodies ('ice balls') comprising a solid rock nucleus

ACETYLENE DREAMS

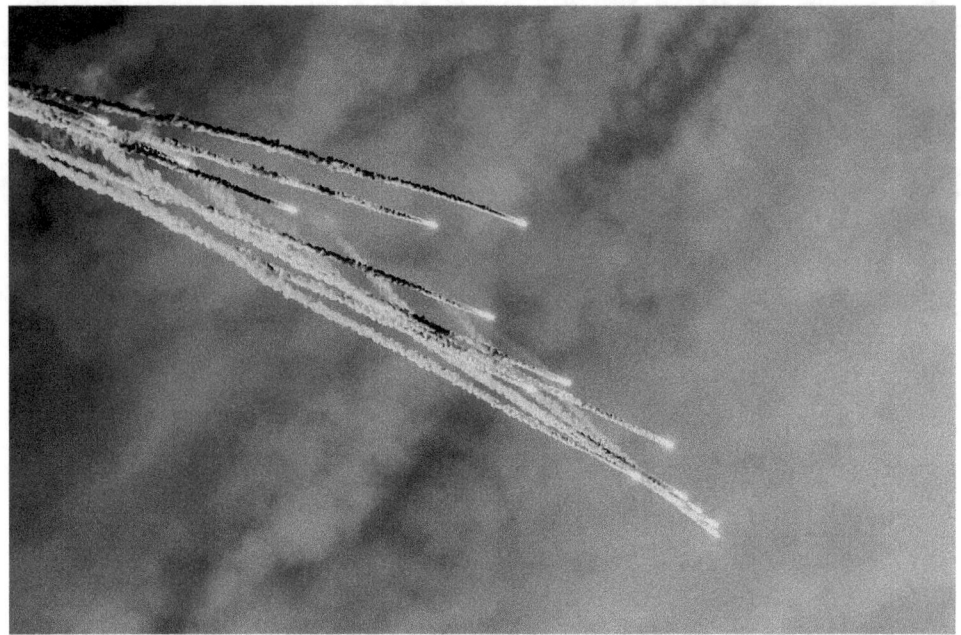

Figure 38: Disintegration (© Shutterstock)

enclosed in a mantle of ice; the ice evaporates when it gets close enough to the Sun. This forms a luminous gaseous *coma* around the core and releases frozen gases and dust into one or more comet tails, thus becoming readily visible as their orbits bring them close enough.

For simplicity, consider meteors as 'fragments of other worlds' or survivors of the universe's formation. What is most impressive about meteors and any remaining meteorite is the spectacular and sometimes catastrophic passage and resultant impact collision with Earth.

As a descending meteor rapidly traverses the upper atmosphere, glowing material disintegrates due to extreme heat and vaporisation, sometimes resulting in an extraordinary visual display. 'Depending upon their size, speed and composition, some fireballs (extremely bright meteors) may explode when striking the atmosphere, producing many fragments.'[5]

Although best estimates indicate that more than 500,000 fireballs may occur every year, and several thousand meteors of fireball magnitude appear daily in the Earth's atmosphere, most go unnoticed, as they pass over the ocean, or occur in daylight.⁶ Few attain the spectacular status of a *bolide* (from the Greek *bolis* meaning 'missile') that explodes with loud sonic booms heard on the ground below.

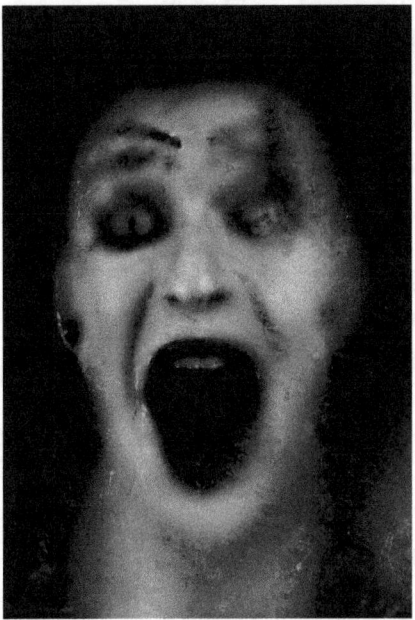

Figure 39: Fireball Shock (© Shutterstock)

To gauge the devastation caused by such rare events, the most recent supersonic exploding meteor occurred near the Podkamennaya Tunguska River, in a sparsely population region of Russia, on 30 June 1908. It resulted in the levelling of an 80m swathe of trees over 2,150 square kilometres. The meteor was believed to have exploded near the Earth's surface 'producing a fireball and releasing energy equivalent to 185 Hiroshima bombs'.[7]

Far more disastrous effects can occur from direct impact craters, as evidenced from the Vredefort Crater in the Free State province of South Africa. This is the world's largest verified terrestrial impact structure, created over an estimated two billion years ago, with the original crater measured at around 300 kilometres diameter (now considerably eroded).[8]

The asteroid or meteor that gouged this depression in the Earth's crust was estimated at a mere 10 -15 kilometres in diameter.[9]

Figure 40: Meteorite Impact Crater (© depositphotos)

For another terrifying experience, consider the ominous meteor shower involving multiple simultaneous aerial strikes. Often the result of cosmic debris, including minute dust particles from passing comets, these meteor 'streams' descend to Earth *en masse.*

Shower meteors are not sporadic, with their time and place of appearance relatively predictable; '… they come from comet dust, small bodies shed by comets and strewn like seeds along comet orbits … A comet does not deposit dust uniformly along its orbit … Instead, it deposits the dust in spurts'.[10]

Figure 41: Meteor Shower (© depositphotos)

As the meteoritic storm approaches, one might think that 'The moon is dark, and the gods dance in the night; there is terror in the sky…'[11]

****

The world's greatest meteor shower, known as 'the night the stars fell like rain' or the Leonid meteor shower, occurred on the night of 12-13 November 1833. This spectacular celestial meteor tempest was associated with the passing comet Tempel-Tuttle and subsequently named Leonid, as it appeared to originate from a point within the Leo constellation.

As the Earth circles the Sun, it passes through various meteor streams, resulting in numerous meteor storms at the same time each year. The first anecdotal record of this particular annual event was originally made as early as 899 A.D.[12] or 902 A.D. by Chinese astronomers and observers, as the Earth passed through the comet's orbit.[13]

The conflicting dates were probably two separate comets recorded in 898 A.D. or 899 A.D., and another described in 902 A.D. as 'a comet appeared with its tail to the east, and continued visible for 40 days.'[14] Such events intensified dramatically once about every 33 years, when the comet's orbit around the Sun took it closest to the Earth.

In late 1833 the comet was as close to the planet as ever before, event described as '… the sky was scored in every direction with shining tracks and illuminated with majestic fireballs… quite beyond counting… 240,000 must have been visible during the nine hours they continued to fall'.[15]

Only the tremendous meteor shower of 17 November 1966 would rival such a phenomenon.

The returning comet named P(Parent)/Tempel-Tuttle and rediscovered as Comet 1965 IV had passed closer to Earth's orbit than any comet since 1833, and because of it '…within just two hours, observed rates increased from about 40 [Leonids] per hour…to as much as 40 per second!'[16]

'We saw a rain of meteors turn into a hail of meteors and finally a storm of meteors too numerous to count,' according to one eyewitness named Charles Capen, who observed it in the San Gabriel Mountains of Southern

ACETYLENE DREAMS

California.[17]

*****

Recurring major meteor showers that occur periodically can vary substantially in numbers from year to year, although 'several showers recorded in the last couple of centuries have produced above 100,000 meteors per hour, reportedly lighting the sky and falling near the rate of a snowstorm.'[18] 'Shooting stars' commonly observed in the atmosphere are often the result of tiny space dust burning up as the planet passes through major celestial dust belts.

Although the Earth's atmosphere is subjected to space rock debris and dust burning up many times daily, in quantities estimated as considerable tonnes each year, the likelihood of meteorite impact is small.

It has been concluded that even major catastrophic impact events from substantially larger objects (likely to affect populations and climate) '…happen about once every thousand years' (when it comes to events that may affect a city) or '…happen every 300,000 years'[19] (in the case of catastrophes that could significantly alter Earth's climate).

So, best to heed the wise words by the 19th century poet Sabine Baring-Gould, as extracted from *Now the Day is Over* (1867) and retire early, rather than worry about all those shooting stars:

> 'Now the day is over,
> Night is drawing nigh,
> Shadows of the evening
> Steal across the sky.
>
> Now the darkness gathers,
> Stars begin to peep,
> Birds and beasts and flowers
> Soon will be asleep …'[20]

COSMIC MESSENGERS

Figure 42: Nightfall (© iStock)

UNIVERSAL STARDUST

That is what all creatures great and small are made of. Leftover stardust. An atom exploded, and all the dust became the planets, the stars… and us. That's all anything amounts to.[1]

Jodi Lynn Anderson
May Bird Among the Stars (2006)

Figure 43: Stardust Trails (© iStock)

UNIVERSAL STARDUST

Stardust can be very complex interstitial matter, particularly if involved in constructing the universe from the beginning, as proposed by children's authors Ian Billings and Chris White in some relevant parts of their poem *How To Build Your Own Universe* (2011):

> '... First you need an empty space
> infinity long is just the place
> then you simply have to scatter
> a million tons of cosmic matter.
>
> Make some atoms very small
> till you can't see them at all.
> Next stir in a trillion masses
> of functionally inert gases.
>
> Then you merely have to glue
> up a zillion stars or two.
> Next you sprinkle in the mix
> The Laws of Thermodynamics ...
>
> Now to start your planetary motion
> what you need's a big explosion ...
>
> ...That really got your worlds revolving
> Look right there – that's life evolving.
> Count you still have all your spheres
> then cool for thirteen billion years ...'[2]

Now that the universe has been created, it would be most appropriate to populate these worlds. So many choices and variations on a theme are possible, given the plethora of atoms and molecules available in the cosmos. 'A micrometer-size particle of stardust is made of billions of atoms.'[3] Now, that is an impressive set of numbers for any life-form building blocks.

ACETYLENE DREAMS

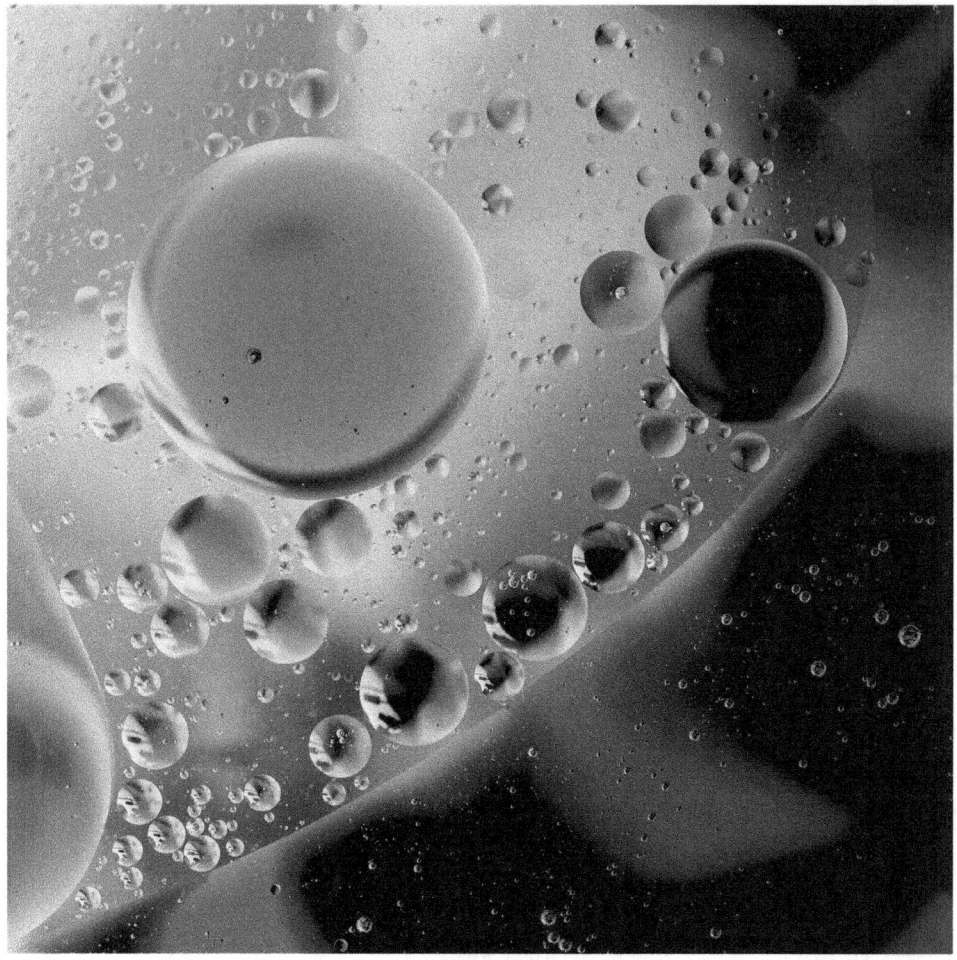

Figure 44: The Beginning(© iStock)

In the case of our home planet, I wonder how other life forms might come to view us. One perspective is provided in the following excerpt from the children's poem *Welcome To Earth* (2011):

> 'Greetings to you Earthlings
> Please don't call the police.
> For although I am an alien
> Chill out! I come in peace!
>
> I've been among you a week or two

Having a look round the place
And one thing I've learnt about humans is
You're not half a funny race! …

…Up in space my ship is faster than light
Zipping from place to place
Down here it takes hours to get anywhere
There are no speed cameras in space …

… On my world we have many fine foods
So much choice – I lick my green lips!
Here on Earth it seems you'll eat anything
As long as it's served up with chips…'[4]

Figure 45: The End (© iStock)

ON A CLEAR DAY

Give me the long, straight road before me,
   A clear, cold day with a nipping air,
Tall, bare trees to run on beside me,
   A heart that is light and free from care.
Then let me go! – I care not whither
   My feet may lead, for my spirit shall be
Free as the brook that flows to the river,
   Free as the river that flows to the sea.[1]

Olive Runner
Freedom (1918)

Figure 46: I Can See Forever (© Shutterstock)

ON A CLEAR DAY

The early 20th century short poem *Freedom* by American poet Olive Runner provides a distinctive signpost for those daring to dream of what lies ahead. On such a clear day with a never-ending view to the horizon, your imagination could so easily take hold and transport you to unknown distant places, and to other times.

As the famous and influential American writer Howard Phillips Lovecraft so eloquently stated in 1921:

> 'Pleasure to me is wonder – the unexplored, the unexpected, the thing that is hidden and the changeless thing that lurks behind superficial mutability. To trace the remote in the immediate; the eternal in the ephemeral; the past in the present; the infinite in the finite; these are to me the springs of delight and beauty.'[2]

For those among us who wonder if it is actually worthwhile to seek new horizons and directions, a sobering thought from the 1922 poem by American Sara Teasdale, *Hide and Seek*:

> 'When I was a child we played sometimes in the dark;
> Hide and seek in the dark is a terrible game,
> With the nerves pulled tight in fear of the stealthy seeker,
> With the brief exultance, and the blood in the veins like flame.
>
> Now I see that life is a game in the dark,
> A groping in shadows, a brief exultance, a dread
> Of what may crouch beside us or lurk behind us,
> A leaving of what we want to say unsaid,
> Sure of one thing only, a long sleep
> When the game is over and we are put to bed.[3]

If there is one overriding attraction in a grandiose view of a spectacular scenery, it has to be the discernible silence that often pervades such settings. For example, if you find yourself admiring a magnificent forest, or an extensive valley of monumental cliffs and canyons, the silence may become overwhelming, thus adding to the subtle grandeur of the view.

Figure 47: The Endless View (© depositphotos)

American Norton Juster, author of several popular children's books, certainly experienced the many facets of silence, as indicated in his 1961 novel, *The Phantom Tollbooth*:

> 'Have you ever heard the wonderful silence just before the dawn?' she enquired. 'Or the quiet and calm just as a storm ends? Or perhaps you know the silence when you haven't the answer to a question you've been asked, or the hush of a country road at night, or the expectant pause of a room full of people when someone is just about to speak, or, most beautiful of all, the moment after the door closes and you're all alone in the whole house? Each one is different, you know, and all very beautiful, if you listen carefully.'[4]

ON A CLEAR DAY

Silence should never be taken for granted, because without respite from the daily turmoil of incessant noise and resultant personal stress, the opportunities for tranquil reflection can be extremely limited.

This is quite obvious at dusk, when birds retreat from the rigours of surviving in the wild to seek sanctuary for the night. Peace and serenity reigns, until their raucous awakening just before dawn, when they resume the daily struggle.

Now add the final element to the endless landscape's fabric – that of desolation and emptiness, with only the subtle yet grim imagery of rusted, abandoned machinery for stark contrast.

Figure 48: Not Coming Back (© iStock)

Unending, serene, lonely, and perhaps symbolic of so many of our acetylene dreams.

REQUIEM FOR A DREAMER

**There's only one place I want to go
and it's to all the places I've never been.**

Nikki Rowe
Once a Girl, Now a Woman

A lonely walk along a windswept beach on a wintry day in the rain; you feel the chilly freshness of the passing storm, the salty air stinging your eyes and crusting your face, and the wet sand trodden underfoot.

An early morning stroll through the mists of a towering forest in the mountains, resplendent in blossoms and the echoes of noisy birdlife; a creeping dampness of thick fog is about to envelop you as the walk continues deeper into the forest.

A calm, silent night shattered only by the distant shrill whistle of a steam train passing in the dark, and the sight of a solitary shooting star flashing briefly overhead.

These are but a few dream experiences that may occur to any of us, given the right circumstances.

New Zealand poet Robert Murray Smith readily identifies with dreams in

Figure 49: Tropical Isle at Sea (© depositphotos)

his contemporary work *Dream On, Dream More* (2018):

> 'Run into the night of dreams,
> For dreams are nights of
> Starlight.
>
> Into the past all lies, passing
> Dreams through those slivers
> Unseen.
>
> To see a dream is to open life
> Where no one has ever
> Been.
>
> Dream on, dream more, open those
> Doors where we can see much
> More.'[1]

The world of dreams is an ephemeral realm of transient ideas and vivid imagination. The key is to always clearly distinguish between fanciful dreams and the relatively harsh reality of life.

ACETYLENE DREAMS

The following evocative excerpt from Ashley L. May's 2006 poem *A Bed of Clouds* highlights this important message:

> 'I sleep in the clouds, dream in the sky,
> I'll keep dreaming as life passes me by,
> I think my dreams keep me sane,
> I dream of happiness, a life without pain,
>
> Some people say I'm stuck in this place,
> and I'll never go anywhere,
> but in my dreams I've already been there,
> I know some day I'll have to wake up, …'[2]

Figure 50: Am I Still Dreaming? (© iStock)

Above all else, dreaming takes you halfway between the immediate and the imaginative, between the present and a distant temporary realm, and ultimately into the unknown and the uncertainty of awakening.

English poet Algernon Charles Swinburne embraced these possibilities in a salient part of his lengthy 1866 poem *The Garden of Proserpine*:

'Here, where the world is quiet;
Here, where all trouble seems
Dead winds' and spent waves' riot
In doubtful dreams of dreams;
I watch the green field growing
For reaping folk and sowing,
For harvest-time and mowing,
A sleepy world of streams…

… Then star nor sun shall waken,
Nor any change of light
Nor sounds of water shaken,
Nor any sound or sight:
Nor wintry leaves nor vernal,
Nor days nor things diurnal;
Only the sleep eternal
In an eternal night.'[3]

Figure 51: Finding Your Way (© depositphotos)

Acetylene Dreams – these are our dreams, our personal journey, and the eventual destination attained by each of us.

REFERENCES

CHAPTER 1: The Wonder of Acetylene

1. Young, Neil, Crazy Horse, *My My, Hey Hey (Out of the Blue)* and *Hey, Hey, My My (Into the Black)*, Single 45 RPM record, Reprise Label, California, USA, Recorded 1978, Released 27 August 1979.

2. Arian Gas, 'Acetylene Gas', https://www.ariangas.com/en/product/acetylene-gas. Accessed 18 June 2018.

3. Tech-FAQ, 'Acetylene', http://www.tech-faq.com/acetylene-torch.html, Retrieved 22 July 2018.

4. Teasdale, Sara, 'The House of Dreams', in *Sonnets to Duse: and other Poems*, 1st Ed., 1907, p.43.

5. Meyer, Stephenie, Twilight #1, *twilight*, 2005, p.233.

CHAPTER 2: Gargoyles

1. Sheridan, R., and Ross, A., 'Glaring Creatures', in *Gargoyles and Grotesques: Paganism in the Medieval Church*, 1975, pp.57-8.

2. Hargreaves, J., *Hargreaves New Illustrated Bestiary*, 1990, p.51.

3. 'Gargle' origin and meaning, in *Online Etymology Dictionary*, Retrieved 18 June 2018, https://www.etymonline.com/word/gargle

4. Benton, J., *Holy Terrors: Gargoyles on Medieval Buildings*, 1st Ed., 1997, pp.11-12.

5. Varner, G.R., 'Grotesques & Green Men', in *Gargoyles, Grotesques & Green Men: Ancient Symbolism in European and American Architecture*, 2008, p.39.

6. ibid., 'Gargoyles and the Church', p.32.

REFERENCES

7. Tschen-Emmons, *Artifacts from Medieval Europe: Daily Life Through Artifacts*, 2015, p.72.

8. Sheridan and Ross, op.cit., p.46

9. Benton, op.cit., p.44.

10. Verana, 'Guardians', *Gargoyle Poems*, https://pucksplace.artchicks.org/aerie/poems.htm. Retrieved 20 June 2018.

11. Benton, op.cit., p.15.

CHAPTER 3: Persona

1. Varakis-Martin, Angeliki, Review of *Mask & Performance In Greek Tragedy:From Ancient Festival To Modern Experimentation* by Wiles, David, https://kar.kent.ac.uk/12969/ Theatre Research International, University of Kent, Great Britain, 2008, p.325.

2. Korsi, 'Did the Egyptian Gods have Animal Heads?, in *Return of the Space Gods*, 14 November 2009, https://returnofthespacegods.wordpress.com/2009/11/14/did-the-egyptian-gods-have-animal-heads/ Retrieved 22 June 2018.

CHAPTER 4: Light and Darkness

1. Thoreau, Chp XVIII 'Conclusion', in *Walden*, 1854 (Published 1892), p.502.

2. Goldstein, J., 'Clowning Basics', in *101 Amazing Facts About Clowns*, 2017, p.5.

3. ibid., 'Bad Clowning', pp.15-16.

4. Roberts, N., 'Prologue', in *Charmed*, 1992.

CHAPTER 5: Fashionista

1. Geczy, A.,'Fashion Dolls', in *The Artificial Body In Fashion And Art: Marionettes, Models and Mannequins*, 2017, pp.91-92.

2. ibid., p.90.

3. Encyclopedia of Clothing and Fashion, 'Mannequins', https://www.encyclopedia.com/fashion/encyclopedias-almanacs-transcripts-and-maps/mannequins, Retrieved 28 June 2018.

4. Brownie, B., 'Mangled mannequins – What happened to shop-window

dummies?', in *The Guardian (Australian Ed.,)* Fashion, 17 August, 2013, p.146.

CHAPTER 6: Dolls

1. Leven, Mel A. (Song Writer), 'Are My Ears On Straight?', *Montclare Music*, 'B' Side of single record *I Want a Hippopotamus for Christmas* by Columbia, performed by Gayla Peevey, Released 11 November 1953, in "Christmas Music Countdown: Day 9.5", The Portland Mercury, 15 December 2010.

2. Smith, M., 'Introduction', in *The Erotic Doll: A Modern Fetish*, 2014, p.9.

3. ibid., p.10.

4 Ashic, A.K., *Poetry*, May 2015, Section 2.

5. Bach, J., *The Warner Collector's Guide to Dolls*, 1982, pp.79-86.

6. Kingsley, C., *The Water-Babies*, 1922, p.167.

7. Bach, 'Character Doll', op.cit., p.136

CHAPTER 7: The Talking Dummy

1. 'Caesar and Me', *The Twilight Zone: The Original Series (1959-1964)*, Season 5, Episode 28, originally aired 10 April 1964, https://en.wikipedia.org/wiki/ Caesar_and_Me. Accessed 3 July 2018.

2. Lincoln, Marshall L., 'Look Inside a Dummy's Head', in *Popular Mechanics*, Issue December 1954, pp.154-57.

3.'The Dummy', *The Twilight Zone: The Original Series (1959-1964)*, Season 3, Episode 33, originally aired 4 May 1962, https://en.wikipedia.org/wiki/ The_Dummy. Accessed 3 July 2018.

4. Stevenson, R.L., *A Child's Garden of Verses*, 1922 Edition, p.38.

5. Schindler, G., *Ventriloquism: Magic with Your Voice*, 1979, p.4.

6. ibid., p.120.

CHAPTER 8: Someone Else

1. 'Mask' origin and meaning, in *Online Etymology Dictionary*, Retrieved 4 July 2018, https://www.etymonline.com/word/mask.

REFERENCES

2. Carroll, L., 'Jabberwocky', in *Through The Looking Glass And What Alice Found There*, 1871, p.22 (Poem Excerpt).

CHAPTER 9: The Fog Of War

1. Owen ,W., 'Dulce et Decorum Est (It is sweet and honourable …)', in *Wilfred Owen: War Poems and Others*, 1973 (Originally published posthumously 1920).

2. Grenfell, Julian, 'Into Battle', in *Poetry of the First World War*, 1988, pp.23-5 (Poem Excerpt).

3. Ward, A., 'Military Equipment', in *The Beginner's Guide to Wartime Collectibles*, 2013, p.44.

4. Horn, Leslie, *This WWII Mickey Mouse Gas Mask Was Supposed To Be Less Creepy Somehow*, 25 June, 2013, https://www.gizmodo.com.au/2013/06/this-wwii-mickey-mouse-gas-mask-was-supposed-to-be-less-creepy-somehow/. Accessed 5 July 2018.

5. Lovecraft, H.P., 'The Call of Cthulhu', in *Weird Tales* Magazine, vol.11, no.2, February 1928, Chapter 1. The Horror in Clay.

CHAPTER 10: Cosmic Messengers

1. Teasdale, S., 'The Falling Star', in *Stars To-Night: Verses New and Old for Boys and Girls*, 1st Ed., 1930; Republished in Mirror of the Heart: Poems of Sara Teasdale, William Drake (ed.), 1984, p.119.

2. Wikipedia encyclopedia, 'Meteor History', in *Meteoroid*, 26 June 2018, https://en.wikipedia.org/wiki/Meteoroid, Accessed 13 July 2018.

3. Golia, M.,'Fallen Gods',in *Meteorite: Nature and Culture*, 2015, p. 55.

4. Norton, O.R.,'Meteor', in *The Cambridge Encyclopedia of Meteorites*, p.344.

5. Golia, M., op.cit., 'Introduction', pp. 8-9.

6. American Meteor Society, *Fireball FAQs*, https://www.amsmeteors.org/fireballs/faqf/#16, Accessed 13 July 2018.

7. Schultz, Colin, 'The Last Massive Exploding Meteor Hit Earth in 1908, Leveling 800 Square Miles of Forrest', *Smart News, Smithsonian.com.*, 15 February 2013, https://www.smithsonianmag.com/smart-news/the-last-

massive-exploding-meteor-hit-earth-in-1908-leveling-800-square-miles-of-forest-18916251/

8. Norton, op.cit., 'Impact Cratering in the Solar System', p.277.

9. Hartebeesthoek Radio Astronomy Observatory, *Deep Impact – The Vredefort Dome*, 14 July 2005, Accessed 15 July 2018.

10. Norton, op.cit., 'Shower Meteors', pp. 12-13.

11. Lovecraft, *The Other Gods*, 1933, p.37.

12. Kwok, 'Rocks and Dust in the Planetary Neighborhood', in *Stardust: The Cosmic Seeds of Life*, 2013, p.14.

13. Leonid MAC, *Brief history of the Leonid Shower*, https://leonid.arc.nasa.gov/history.html Accessed 15 July 2018.

14. Brewster (ed.), 'A Chronological Table from the Creation of the World to the Year 1813', in *The Edinburgh Encyclopædia*, vol.VI, William Blackwood, 1830, p.434.

15. Clerke, Agnes, 'Recent Comets', in *A Popular History of Astronomy during the Nineteenth Century*, Part II, Chp. X, 1893, pp.398-99 [Arago, *Annuaire*, 1836, p.294].

16. Leonid MAC, op.cit., *Comet P/Tempel-Tuttle Rediscovered (1965)*, Accessed 16 July 2018.

17. Rao, Joe, *The Leonids: King of the Meteor Showers*, 1998, http://genealogytrails.com/ill/stars.htm, Accessed 16 July 2018.

18. Elkins-Tanton, 'Meteor Showers', in *Asteroids, Meteorites, and Comets*, 2006, p.153.

19. Kusky, T., ' Hazards of Impacts and Mitigating the Dangers of Future Impacts, in *Asteroids and Meteorites: Catastrophic Collisions with Earth*, 2009, pp.105-106.

20. Baring-Gould, Sabine, 'Now the Day is Over' (originally published 16 September 1867 *The Church Times*), in *The Oxford Book of Children's verse*, 1973, p.238.

CHAPTER 11: Universal Stardust

1. Anderson, J.L., 'Chapter 10 -The Stranger', in *May Bird Among the Stars*, Book Two, 2006, p.93.

REFERENCES

2. Billings, I., and White, C., 'How To Build Your Own Universe', in *Space Rocks! A Universe Of Looney Verse*, 2011, p.44.

3. Kwok, S., 'Stars as Molecular Factories', in *Stardust: The Cosmic Seeds of Life*, 2013, p.81.

4. Billings and White, op.cit.,'Welcome to Earth', pp.84-5.

CHAPTER 12: On A Clear Day

1. Runner, O., 'Freedom', in *Poetry: A Magazine of Verse*, September 1918, p.302. https://archive.org/details/jstor-20571813, Retrieved 11 July 2018.

2. Lovecraft, H.P., Joshi, S.T. (ed.),'The Defence Remains Opens!' (April 1921), in *In Defence of Dagon*, 1st Ed.,Necronomicon Press, Rhode Island, USA, June 1985.

3. Drake, 'Hide and Seek' previously unpublished 1922 poem in Beinecke Rare Book and Manuscript Library, Yale University, in *Mirror of the Heart: Poems of Sara Teasdale*, 1984, p.92.

4. Juster and Feiffer, 'The Silent Valley', in *The Phantom Tollbooth*, 1st Ed., 1961, pp.151-2.

CHAPTER 13: Requiem For A Dreamer

1. Murray-Smith, Robert, *Dream On, Dream More*, Poem Hunter, March 2018, https://www.poemhunter.com › Poems › Dream On Dream More, Retrieved 29 July 2018.

2. May, Ashley L., *A Bed Of Clouds*, February 2006, familyfriend Poems, https://www.familyfriendpoems.com/poem/life-and-dreams-poem, Accessed 30 July 2018.

3. Swinburne, A.C., 'The Garden of Proserpine', in *Poems and Ballads*, First Series,1866, pp.196-9.

BIBLIOGRAPHY

Anderson, Jodi Lynn, *May Bird Among the Stars*, Book Two, Scholastic Book Services, New York, United Kingdom, November 2006.

Ashic, A.K., *Poetry*, eBook, Lulu Press, 2015.

Bach, Jean, *The Warner Collector's Guide to Dolls*, Main Street Press, New York, USA, 1982.

Benton, Janetta, *Holy Terrors: Gargoyles on Medieval Buildings*, 1st Ed., Abbeville Press, New York, USA, 1997.

Billings, Ian, and White, Chris, *Space Rocks! A Universe Of Looney Verse*, Caboodle Books Ltd, Great Britain, 2011.

Brewster, David, Sir (ed.), *The Edinburgh Encyclopaedia*, vol.VI, William Blackwood, 1830.

Carroll, Lewis, *Through The Looking Glass And What Alice Found There*, 1st Ed., Macmillan & Co., London, December 1871.

Clerke, Agnes Mary, *A Popular History of Astronomy during the Nineteenth Century*, 3rd Ed., Adam and Charles Black, London, 1893.

Drake, William (ed.), *Mirror of the Heart: Poems of Sara Teasdale*, Macmillan Publishing, New York, Collier Macmillan, London, 1984.

Elkins-Tanton, Linda T., *Asteroids, Meteorites, and Comets*, Chelsea House, New York, USA, 2006.

Geczy, Adam, *The Artificial Body In Fashion And Art: Marionettes, Models and Mannequins*, Bloomsbury Publishing, New York & London, 2017.

Goldstein, Jack, *101 Amazing Facts About Clowns*, 1st Ed., Andrews UK

BIBLIOGRAPHY

Limited, Luton, Bedfordshire, United Kingdom, 2017.

Golia, Maria, *Meteorite: Nature and Culture*, Reaktion Books, London, UK, 2015.

Hargreaves, Joyce, *Hargreaves New Illustrated Bestiary*, Gothic Image Publications, Great Britain, 1990.

Hudson, Edward, *Poetry of the First World War*, Wayland Publishers, Hove, East Sussex, UK, 1988.

Juster, Norton and Feiffer, Jules (Illustrator), *The Phantom Tollbooth*, 1st Ed., Epstein and Carroll Associates Inc., USA, September 1961.

Kingsley, Charles, *The Water-Babies: A Fairy Tale for a Land-Baby*, McMillan & Company, London, Great Britain, 1922.

Kusky, Timothy, Ph.D., *Asteroids and Meteorites: Catastrophic Collisions with Earth*, Facts On File Inc., New York, USA, 2009.

Kwok, Sun, *Stardust: The Cosmic Seeds of Life*, Springer-Verlag Berlin and Heidleberg, GmbH & Co KG, Germany, 2013.

Lovecraft, Howard Phillips, 'The Call of Cthulhu', *Weird Tales: The Unique Magazine*, vol.II, no.2, Rural Publishing Corporation, Chicago, USA, Issue February 1928.

Lovecraft, Howard Phillips, 'The Other Gods', *The Fantasy Fan*, vol.1 No.3, November 1933.

Lovecraft, Howard Phillips, *In Defence of Dagon*, Necronomicon Press, 1985.

Meyer, Stephenie. *twilight*, Little, Brown and Company, New York, USA, October 2005.

Monroe, Harriet (Ed.), *Poetry: A Magazine of Verse*, vol. XII, no.VI, *Poetry* magazine, Chicago, USA, September 1918.

Norton, O. Richard, *The Cambridge Encyclopedia of Meteorites*, Cambridge University Press, Cambridge UK, 2002.

Opie, Iona and Opie, Peter, *The Oxford Book of Children's verse*, Clarendon Press, Oxford, Great Britain, 1973.

Owen, Wilfred, Hibberd, Dominic (ed.), *Wilfred Owen: War Poems and Others*, Chatto and Windus, London, UK, 1973.

Roberts, Nora, *Charmed, (The Donovan Legacy, #3)*, 1st Ed., Harlequin, London, November 1992.

Rowe, Nikki, *Once a Girl, Now a Woman*, Balboa Press, Australia, June 2013.

Sheridan, Ronald, and Ross, Anne, *Gargoyles and Grotesques: Paganism in the Medieval Church*, David & Charles (Holdings) Ltd, Newton Abbot, Devon, England, 1975.

Schindler, George, *Ventriloquism: Magic with Your Voice*, Dover Publications, Mineola, New York, USA,1979.

Stevenson, Robert Louis, *A Child's Garden of Verses*, 1st Ed., Longhaus, Green & Co, London, Great Britain, 1885.

Smith, Marquard, *The Erotic Doll: A Modern Fetish*, Yale University Press, New Haven and London, 2014.

Swinburne, Algernon Charles, *Poems and Ballads*, First Series, Savill and Edwards, London, 1866.

Taylor, Lenore (ed.), *The Guardian newspaper*, Issue 17 August 2013, Guardian News and Medial Limited, Australia, 2013.

Teasdale, Sara, *Sonnets to Duse: and other Poems*, The Poet Lore Company, Boston, USA, 1907.

Teasdale, Sara, *Stars To-Night: Verses New and Old for Boys and Girls*, 1st Ed., The Macmillan Company, New York, USA, 1930.

Thoreau, Henry D., *Walden*, Vol.II, The Riverside Press, Cambridge, USA, 1892.

Tschen-Emmons, James B., *Artifacts from Medieval Europe: Daily Life Through Artifacts*, ABC-CLIO, LLC, California, USA, 2015.

Varner, Gary, Gargoyles, *Gargoyles & Green Men: Ancient Symbolism in European and American Architecture*, 2nd Ed., Lulu Press, USA, 2008.

Ward, Arthur, *The Beginner's Guide to Wartime Collectibles,* Pen & Sword Military, Barnsley, South Yorkshire, Great Britain, 2013.

Wiles, David, *Mask & Performance In Greek Tragedy: From Ancient Festival To Modern Experimentation*, Cambridge University Press, Cambridge, 2007.

BIBLIOGRAPHY

Windsor, Jnr., H.H., (ed.), *Popular Mechanics Magazine*, Issue December 1954, Popular Mechanics Company, Chicago, USA, 1954.

Yonnet, Jacques, *Rue des Maléfices: Chronique secrete d'une ville* (originally *Enchantements sur Paris*), Denoël, Paris, France, 1954.

ABOUT THE AUTHOR

Figure 52: Many Dreams (© iStock)

Simon King is an emerging Australian author who has already published five books:

Crocodiles and Cocktails: A Decade of Adventure at the Kimberley Frontier

Witchcraft, Whispers, Shadows and Strange Sights: A Journey into the Unknown and Unexpected

ABOUT THE AUTHOR

Marbles, Marella Jubes and Milk Bottles: My Golden Years of Australian Childhood

Robot Awakening: The Time of Artificial Life

On The Edge: Extreme Life

Each book encompasses different aspects of life's journey, and engages many interesting historical and contemporary perspectives.

His literary work can be reviewed on the website: **www.sdkauthor.com**.

Simon's interest in exploring the complexities of the human identity through comparison with everyday cultural objects, such as dolls, mannequins and even gargoyles provides an interesting insight into what defines us. This book provides some intriguing answers to such matters, inclusive of the relevance of our imaginative dreams.

www.ingramcontent.com/pod-product-compliance
Lightning Source LLC
Chambersburg PA
CBHW050604300426
44112CB00013B/2070